On It, Phonics! Consonant Blends

We Clap in Class

The CL Blend

By Connor Stratton

level 1
little blue readers

www.littlebluehousebooks.com

Little Blue House is distributed by North Star Editions:
sales@northstareditions.com | 888-417-0195

Produced for Little Blue House by Red Line Editorial.

Reading Consultant: Andrew P. Johnson, PhD, Distinguished Faculty Scholar and Professor of Literacy Instruction, Minnesota State University, Mankato

Photographs ©: iStockphoto, cover, 5 (clap), 5 (clay), 5 (clean), 5 (climb), 5 (clock), 5 (cloud), 9 (top), 9 (bottom), 11, 13 (top), 13 (bottom), 15, 23; Shutterstock Images, 5 (class), 6, 17, 19, 21

Library of Congress Control Number: 2023910302

ISBN
978-1-64619-934-1 (hardcover)
978-1-64619-952-5 (paperback)
978-1-64619-986-0 (ebook pdf)
978-1-64619-970-9 (hosted ebook)

Printed in the United States of America
Mankato, MN
102023

About the Author

Connor Stratton writes and edits nonfiction children's books. He lives in Minnesota.

Table of Contents

Consultant Note

"On It, Phonics!" is designed to reinforce vowel sounds, beginning blends, and sight words and to provide reading practice for young readers. Books like these are one important part of a comprehensive literacy program for students at emergent and beginning levels. "On It, Phonics!" should be used with other high-quality children's books. Instructors and parents are advised to go over the words in the picture glossary before students begin reading, and review the sight words after students finish reading. You can also ask students to go back and identify words with the target letter-sound.

Andrew P. Johnson, PhD,
Distinguished Faculty Scholar and
Professor of Literacy Instruction,
Minnesota State University, Mankato

CL Blend Picture Glossary

clap

class

clay

clean

climb

clock

cloud

class

Class

This is a class.

This is a cloud.

This is a clock.

cloud

clock

We can clap.

clap

We can clean.

We can climb.

clean

climb

We have clay.

clay

We clap in class.

clap

We clean our class.

clean

We climb in class.

climb

We have clay in class.

clay

Sight Words

a
can
have
in
is
our
this
we